MARVIN TERBAN

MAD AS A WET HEN!

And Other Funny Idioms

illustrated by
GIULIO MAESTRO

CLARION BOOKS
TICKNOR & FIELDS: A HOUGHTON MIFFLIN COMPANY
NEW YORK

To my mother hen, Sally Terban,
with love from her chick

Clarion Books
Ticknor & Fields, a Houghton Mifflin Company
Text copyright © 1987 by Marvin Terban
Illustrations copyright © 1987 by Giulio Maestro

Printed in the U.S.A.

Library of Congress Cataloging-in-Publication Data

Terban, Marvin.
Mad as a wet hen!
Summary: Illustrates and explains over 100 common English idioms, in categories
including animals, body parts, and colors.
1. English language—Idioms—Juvenile literature. [1. English language—Idioms.
2. English language—Terms and phrases]
I. Maestro, Giulio, ill.
II. Title.
PE1460.T387 1987   428.1   86-17575
ISBN 0-89919-478-8
Paperback ISBN ISBN 0-89919-479-6

HC P   PA AL 10 9 8 7 6 5 4 3 2

Contents

Introduction

Idioms can be the most confusing part of any language. Idioms are sayings that have hidden meanings. The expressions don't mean exactly what the words say.

People use idioms every day. There are thousands of them. The funny pictures and interesting explanations in this book will help you understand over 130 of the most common idioms in English today. No one knows where all the idioms came from. Even word experts don't agree. This book tells some of the most fascinating origins.

·1·

Animals

Most people love animals—dogs, birds, fish, cats, horses, and even bugs! Many well-known idioms are about animals. Maybe it's because animals often act like people, or people often act like animals. Here are some of the most common animal idioms.

Dogs

1. "This place is **going to the dogs**." It's run-down and needs fixing up.

■ Hundreds of years ago, a dog was a lowly hunting animal who slept on the hard, cold floor. He wasn't loved or fed delicious pet food. Leftover table scraps "went to the dogs." Poor Fido! Today we say that a person or business that's on its way to ruin is "going to the dogs."

2. "These are the **dog days** of summer."
   These are the hottest days of July and August.

   ■ The brightest star in the sky is called Sirius. It's in the constellation called "The Big Dog," so it's called "the dog star." On summer mornings, Sirius rises near the sun. The ancient Romans thought that July and August were so hot because the heat from "the dog star" was added to the heat of the sun. So, they called the hottest days "dog days."

3. "He's **in the doghouse** now."
   He's in disgrace for doing something bad.

   ■ In an old story, a wife was so angry at her husband that she made him sleep in the doghouse. Today a person is "in the doghouse" when he's done something so awful that other people are annoyed with him and don't want him around.

4. "I'm living **a dog's life**."
   I'm working hard and not being treated nicely.

5. "It's **raining cats and dogs!**"
   It's raining very hard and coming down in torrents!

   ■ In old England, there were big holes in the roads. There were also many cats and dogs running around loose. During a heavy rainstorm the holes would fill with water. The cats and dogs sometimes fell into them. So people joked that it was "raining cats and dogs."

6. "You'd better **let sleeping dogs lie**."
   You'd better let things be and not stir up trouble.

7. "It's a **dog eat dog** world out there."
   Everyone is fighting to get what he wants even if it hurts others.

8. "She's the **underdog** in this campaign."
   She's in an inferior position with little power.

VOTE FOR TOP DOG! OR ELSE!

Wolves

9. "She's **a wolf in sheep's clothing**."
   She's an enemy disguised as a friend.

10. "He just likes to **cry wolf**."
   He gives a false warning of danger that isn't there.

■ Aesop, the wonderful storyteller of ancient Greece, told two famous fables about wolves. In the first fable, a wolf disguised himself as a sheep to fool the other sheep and get himself a nice sheep dinner. The trick worked!

In the second story, a mischievous shepherd kept shouting "Wolf!" to fool his neighbors. They kept running from their fields to help him, but it was always a false alarm. When a real wolf appeared, no one paid attention to the shepherd's cries.

11. "They work hard to **keep the wolf from the door**."
They work hard so they'll have enough to eat.

■ Wolves sometimes go a long time without eating, so when they see food, they have big appetites. So, if a wolf comes to your door, keep him away. He'll probably gobble up all your food.

Birds and Fowl

12. "Your **goose is cooked!**"
Your plans are ruined.

■ A fierce enemy once attacked a medieval town. To insult the attackers, the townspeople hung a goose outside the town. The enemy burnt the town down anyway, so they "cooked the goose" of the townspeople.

13. "This is **a wild-goose chase**."
We're chasing something that's not worth anything.

■ A wild goose runs so fast that it's almost impossible to catch. Even if you could grab it, what would you do with it? Someone is on "a wild-goose chase" if he's trying to achieve something difficult that's a big waste of time and energy.

14. **"The early bird catches the worm."**
If you start a job earlier than someone else, you'll succeed.

15. "That's **for the birds**."
    That's foolish and worthless.

16. "He thinks a thousand dollars is **chicken feed**."
    He thinks it's a very small amount of money.

17. "Let's **talk turkey**."
    Let's talk business and get the job done.

■ An American Indian and a Pilgrim went turkey hunting together. At the end of the day they wanted to divide the fowl they'd caught, so they had to "talk turkey."

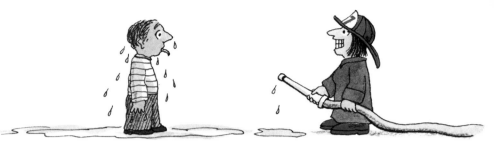

18. "He stopped smoking **cold turkey**."
    He stopped suddenly and without medical aid.

19. "These are **as scarce as hen's teeth**."
    They're very rare and almost impossible to get.

    ■ Hens have no teeth, so what could be scarcer than something that doesn't exist?

20. "He's a **stool pigeon**."
    He tells bad secrets about people to get them into trouble.

    ■ Hunters used to tie a pigeon to a stool and use it as a decoy to attract other pigeons. This "stool pigeon" certainly got the other pigeons into trouble.

21. "She's **as mad as a wet hen!**"
She's furiously angry.

■ A hen doesn't like to get wet. If it does, it flaps its wings wildly to shake the water off. If you saw a wet hen flapping furiously, you'd probably think it was in an insane rage.

22. "The president is a **lame duck**."
He's going out of office and has lost his political power.

■ A politician whose term in office is ending is like a disabled duck, limping lamely and wobbling weakly to the end of his term.

Fish

23. "He's like a **fish out of water**."
    He's out of his proper place and doesn't fit in.

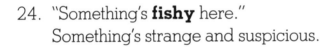

24. "Something's **fishy** here."
    Something's strange and suspicious.

■ Some fishermen/women have reputations for stretching the truth. They'll tell you that a "big fish got away," but actually they didn't catch any fish at all. No wonder we call a suspicious story "fishy"!

Insects

25. "That kid has **ants in his pants**."
    He's so restless, he can't sit still.

    ■ Just imagine a swarm of ants scurrying inside your trousers—while you're wearing them! You'd surely fidget and squirm. Well, when you're nervous, or excited, or jumpy, people say you have "ants in your pants."

26. "That's the **fly in the ointment**."
    That is what's spoiling this whole thing.

27. "You're **stirring up a hornet's nest**."
You're causing a lot of trouble.

28. "Don't **bug** me!"
Don't bother me!

29. "I remember when you were **knee-high to a grasshopper**."
You were extremely young and very short.

■ Even the shortest person in the world stands taller than the knee of a grasshopper. But if a person wants to say that he knew you a long time ago when you were tiny, he might use this idiom.

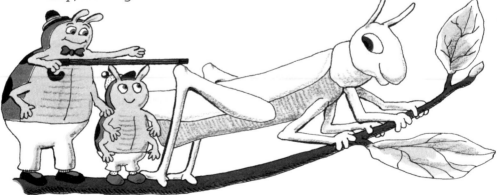

Rodents

30. "Don't **rat** on anyone."
Don't tell secrets about people.

31. "I **smell a rat**."
I'm suspicious. I think something is wrong.

◼ A cat has a sharp nose. A cat can smell a rat even if it can't see it. If you suspect that somebody has done something wrong, even though you can't actually see the bad business, you're like the cat who can smell the rat.

32. "I'm getting out of this **rat race**."
I'm quitting this hectic, confusing job that has no purpose.

◼ Rats are often used in laboratory experiments. They are sometimes placed on treadmills to test their energy. The rats run and run, tire themselves out, and get nowhere. You can see why a person who has a job like that calls it a "rat race."

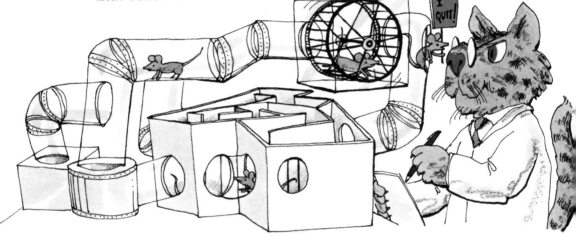

33. "They're **as poor as church mice**."
They're extremely poor.

◼ Mice usually live in cellars or walls. They're not pampered house pets and have to eat leftover food scraps. In this old idiom, the mice who lived in churches had it even worse—there were no pantries in churches and food wasn't usually stored there.

Horses

34. "Get down off your **high horse**."
Stop acting so stuck up and superior.

■ Long ago in royal parades, people of high rank rode high horses. Those people were special. Today if you tell someone to "get down off your high horse" (even if he's standing on the ground), you're telling him to stop acting so snooty. He's not so special.

35. **"Hold your horses!"**
Stop! Wait! Be patient! Control yourself!

■ Long ago this expression meant what it said: Control your team of horses. Don't let them get too excited. Today, few people drive teams of horses, and the idiom means: Control yourself. Don't let yourself get too excited.

36. "Don't **look a gift horse in the mouth**."
    Don't complain if the gift isn't perfect.

    ■ You can often tell the age of a horse by the size and shape of its teeth. If someone gives you a "new" horse, you shouldn't look into its mouth to see if it's an old horse. As a matter of fact, you shouldn't examine any gift too closely for defects.

37. "Well, that's **a horse of a different color**."
    That's a completely different matter.

Bulls

38. "He's like a **bull in a china shop**."
   He's a very clumsy person who breaks lots of things accidentally.

39. "You have to **take the bull by the horns**."
   You have to be brave and do something about this difficult situation.

More Animals

40. "I like to **get his goat**."
   I like to annoy him and get him very angry!

■ Years ago, a goat was put into the stable of a nervous racehorse to make friends with it and keep it calm. But if a dishonest gambler wanted to make the racehorse nervous so that it would lose the race, he would steal the goat.

41. "She's **making a monkey** out of you."
She's making you look foolish.

■ Monkeys are funny. They swing from trees, make faces, and act silly. People love to laugh at them. If you make a person look ridiculous so that others laugh at him, you're "making a monkey" out of him.

Shh!

42. **"Clam up!"**
Be silent! Don't say anything!

43. "That was **the straw that broke the camel's back**."
That was the last little extra trouble that finally made the situation unbearable. (Also known as **the last straw**.)

■ Imagine a camel piled high with heavy goods. One extra tiny piece, like a straw, is placed on top of the others, and the camel's back breaks. Imagine a situation full of troubles. One more small bad thing happens, and everything becomes impossible to bear.

·2·

Body Parts

Our bodies are always with us. We can't get away from them. When people want to use colorful language, they often think of the things closest to them: their faces or hands or other body parts. No wonder so many idioms are about the body from the tops of our heads to the tips of our toes.

Face and Head

44. "Don't believe her. She's **two-faced**." She's dishonest and disloyal.

   ■ A person usually tells you what she thinks by the words that come out of her mouth and the expression on her face. But if the person says one thing and means another, then she has "two faces"—the honest one and the dishonest one.

45. "You'll just have to **face the music** now." You'll have to take your punishment bravely.

46. "She **laughed her head** off."
    She laughed and laughed and laughed and laughed and laughed.

47. "He's **head over heels** in love with her."
    He's totally in love. He's really flipped for her!

48. "His **head is in the clouds**."
    He's in a fantasy world. His mind is lost in dreams.

49. "Now, don't **lose your head** over this."
Don't become too excited and lose your self-control.

■ Your brain is in your head. When your head is in control, you can think things through carefully before acting. But if you start to behave wildly, without thinking, then you've "lost your head," and someone might tell you "to keep your head."

50. "She's trying to **keep her head above water**."
She is trying to stay out of trouble.

51. "He's **in over his head**."
This is beyond his abilities. He's certain to fail.

Eyes

52. "She's **pulling the wool over his eyes**."
She's tricking him.

   ◾ In Europe a long time ago, judges wore huge woolen wigs. Sometimes a judge's wig slipped over his eyes and he couldn't see. A dishonest lawyer who thought he'd fooled a judge might brag that he had "pulled the wool" over the judge's eyes. He had tricked the judge and the judge hadn't noticed.

53. "We **see eye to eye** on this matter."
We agree fully.

54. "I'm **all eyes**."
I'm watching very carefully.

55. "The teacher has **eyes in the back of her head**."
She knows what's happening even when her back is turned.

Nose

56. "Don't **cut off your nose to spite your face**."
Don't harm yourself just to get revenge on someone else.

■ A person can get so angry at another person that he does something foolish and spites, or hurts, himself. Suppose you're angry with someone and won't go to a party because he will be there. Whom would you be hurting? Only yourself, because you'd be missing a good time.

57. "It's **no skin off my nose**."
It doesn't matter to me in the least.

58. "You'll have to **pay through the nose** to get that."
You'll have to pay much too high a price.

59. "Don't **stick your nose into other people's business**."
Don't intrude where you don't belong.

60. "She always **looks down her nose** at us."
She sneers at us and thinks we're worthless.

Mouth

61. "She was **born with a silver spoon in her mouth**."
She was born rich.

■ A baby isn't born with anything in his/her mouth, not even teeth (usually). However, some infants get fed with silver spoons. Since a silver spoon is expensive, a newborn baby with one in his/her mouth might be thought of as rich.

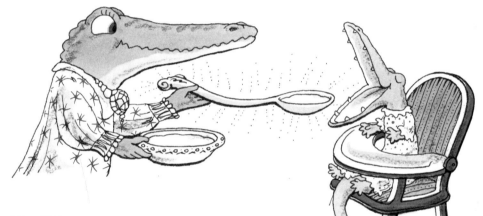

62. "Keep **a stiff upper lip**."
Try to face your troubles bravely.

63. "He escaped **by the skin of his teeth**."
He just barely escaped.

■ What could be thinner than the film on your teeth? If you get out of some danger with very little time or room to spare, you've escaped by "the skin of your teeth."

64. "You'd better **hold your tongue** and **button your lip**."
Stop talking.

65. **"Watch your mouth!"**
Be careful what you say.

66. "The **cat's got her tongue**."
She's so embarrassed or shy that she cannot speak.

Ears

67. "Please **lend me your ear**."
Listen to me.

68. "He's **all ears**."
He's listening very carefully.

69. "He's still **wet behind the ears**."
He's new and inexperienced.

■ When a calf or colt is born, it is wet with birth fluid. Soon it dries off. But there is a little sunken spot behind the ears that is the last place to dry. So anyone "wet behind the ears" is innocent and unsophisticated like a newborn animal.

70. "Let's **play it by ear**."
Let's decide what to do as we go along.

■ Some people can hear a song and play it without studying the notes or reading the music. If you just know what to do in a situation without planning in advance, you're "playing it by ear."

Heart

71. "Don't **eat your heart out** over this."
Don't get weak from being too sad.

72. "She has **a heart of gold**."
She's a kind, generous person.

73. "He **lost his heart** to her."
He fell in love with her.

74. "She has her **heart in her mouth**."
She's extremely nervous.

Neck and Throat

75. "He's **a pain in the neck**."
    He's obnoxious and bothersome.

76. "She **jumped down my throat** when I said that."
    Suddenly she became angry and scolded me severely.

Chest

77. "He got it **off his chest**."
He told someone what was bothering him and then he felt better.

Legs and Toes, Arms and Fingers

78. "He got **cold feet**."
He lost his courage.

79. "Are you **pulling my leg**?"
Are you trying to fool me?

■ Years ago in England, a robber would use a cane or a wire stretched across the sidewalk to catch a person's leg. After the pedestrian fell, he was robbed. Today if someone "pulls your leg," he's just trying to fool you with some kind of trick. He's being a real tease!

80. "Put a little **elbow grease** into this job!"
Work extra-hard.

■ "Elbow grease" is an old slang expression for "sweat." Today we put a little "elbow grease" into any hard job that requires a lot of arm motions like scrubbing, hammering, or sawing. In olden days, a practical joker would send an unsuspecting person to buy a jar of "elbow grease" because there was a tough job to be done.

81. "That **tickles my funny bone**."
That appeals to my sense of humor.

■ In your upper arm is a bone called the "humerus," which sounds like "humorous," which means "funny." The tip of the humerus is your elbow. If you get hit there, you get a tingling sensation, which some people think feels funny. So they call the humerus the "funny bone." When a joke or a situation "tickles our funny bone," we're having fun.

82. "Grandma sure has a **green thumb**."
She has a talent for gardening and knows how to make things grow.

83. "I give that a **thumbs up**."
I approve.

84. **"Thumbs down."**
I disapprove.

■ In ancient Rome, gladiators were fighters. At gladiator contests in the public arenas, the spectators voted on whether the losers of the fights should live or die. They voted with their thumbs. "Thumbs up" was a vote for life. "Thumbs down" meant bad luck for the loser.

85. "He's **all thumbs**."
    He's very clumsy and can't do delicate work.

86. "Come on, everyone, **on your toes!**"
    Be alert and ready for action!

87. "That **costs an arm and a leg!**"
    That's way too expensive and it isn't really worth it.

·3·

Feelings

There are a lot of idioms about strong emotions—feeling happy or sad, getting into trouble, and especially about being angry or making someone angry. The idioms about anger are often about explosions. A person becoming angrier and angrier is like a volcano getting hotter and hotter. What finally happens? Pow! It explodes!

Angry

88. Son is **driving** his father **up the wall**.

89. Daughter is **driving** her mother **nuts**.

90. Uncle is **hot under the collar**.

91. Grandmother is **blowing off steam**.

92. Sister is **blowing her top**.

93. Aunt is **hitting the ceiling**.

94. Brother is **flying off the handle**.

95. Grandpa is **blowing his stack**.

■ The boiler of an old steamboat sometimes over-heated. This caused the smokestack to blow off. A person whose anger is boiling over is like that super-hot steamboat blowing its stack.

Happy and Sad

96. "She's **down in the dumps** today."
    She feels gloomy and depressed.

97. "He's **walking on air**."
    He's overjoyed.

98. "I'm feeling **under the weather**."
    I feel sick.

■ Imagine you're on a ship when a violent storm comes up. The boat begins to toss and your stomach feels queasy. You're feeling "under the weather." An airplane pilot tries to fly his plane above the stormy weather. That will make his passengers feel better.

In Trouble

99. "Oh, oh. We're **in hot water** now."
    We're in very big trouble.

100. "You're **up the creek without a paddle**."
     You're in a hopeless situation and can't do anything about it.

101. "He's **upset the applecart**."
     He's ruined some carefully made plans.

■ A farmer gently picks apples and loads them cautiously into his wagon. He drives slowly down the road to market. Crash! Someone knocks into him and spills all his apples. The farmer's plans are surely ruined.

102. "She's **between the devil and the deep blue sea**."
She's between two equal dangers.

   ■ On the side of old ships there was a heavy plank that supported the guns. It was called "the devil" because it was a dangerous place. If a sailor found himself "between the devil and the deep blue sea," he'd want to get to safety fast.

103. "We're **on thin ice**."
We're risking something dangerous.

104. "He's **behind the eight ball**."
He's out of luck.

   ■ In one game of pool (called "rotation") you have to hit fifteen numbered balls so that they roll into the pockets on the pool table in order. But you have to sink the eight ball last or you lose. If the eight ball is blocking the ball you're aiming for, you're in trouble. You're "behind the eight ball."

·4·

Colors

What a dull world this would be without colors. Black and white skies, trees, and flowers. Dull. Black and white birds, dresses, and toys. Dull. Colors add life to life. And colors often have special meanings and feelings of their own beyond just shades and hues. Think about what the colors mean in the following group of colorful idioms.

105. "I'm **green with envy**."
     I'm very jealous.

106. "Don't **be yellow**!"
     Don't be a coward!

107. "She's **feeling blue**."
She's sad and dejected. She's **down in the dumps**.

108. "When Dad looked, he **saw red**.
He became furious.

109. "I hate all this **red tape**."
I hate these annoying little official delays in a job.

■ Government authorities used to tie up legal documents with red tape. Before you could get any work done, you had to cut all that tape to get the papers you needed. Today any exasperating official procedures that slow down a project are called "red tape."

110. "Let's go out tonight and **paint the town red**."
Let's go out and have a wild time.

■ In olden days, people who were celebrating a good time, like on the Fourth of July or New Year's Eve, would light big bonfires. The flickering light of the bonfires would cast a reddish glow all around, painting the town red.

111. "She's feeling **in the pink**."
She's in good health.

·5·

Food

From breakfast, to midmorning snack, to lunch, to after-school snack, to dinner, to bedtime snack, food is on our minds, in our mouths, or down our stomachs. That probably explains why so many idioms relate to food and eating.

112. "That's **a piece of cake**."
That's very easy to do.

113. "They belong to the **upper crust**."
They're part of the richest, most important people in society.

■ Many years ago, the top slices of bread were served to the nobility. These "upper crusts" were considered the best parts. Today "upper crust" doesn't refer to the bread anymore, but to those in high society who used to eat it.

114. "He's not **worth his salt**."
He's a poor worker and has not earned his salary.

■ Ancient Roman soldiers used part of their pay to buy salt. Salt was hard to get but essential to health. And it made food taste better. A worthless soldier was not worth the salary he was paid to buy himself salt. By the way, the word *salary* comes from the Latin word for salt, *sal*.

115. "Don't **bite off more than you can chew**."
Don't try to do more than you have the time or ability to do.

116. "Well, **that takes the cake!**"
That wins the prize. That beats everything.

■ A cake was often the grand prize in a contest. There was once a "cake walk" contest. Couples walked around a cake with high prancing steps. Judges decided which couple walked with the most graceful or original steps. The winners got to keep the cake!

117. "She always tries to **butter me up**."
She acts very nice to me because she wants something from me.

Yum!

118. "That kid's **eating me out of house and home**."
He's eating so much I'll soon be out of money buying him food.

■ Growing children need a lot of food. Imagine a child who gobbles up everything on the dinner table, devours everything in the refrigerator, and consumes everything in the kitchen cabinets. Of course this story isn't true, but the parents of children who are big eaters often joke, "He's eating me out of house and home!"

119. "They're **going bananas**!"
They're acting silly or ridiculous.

■ Monkeys love bananas. Monkeys often behave in funny ways. They swing wildly from trees and do weird things. Sometimes they eat bananas while being silly. So, a person acting crazy is "going bananas."

120. "She's the **apple of his eye**."
He loves her and treasures her highly.

121. **"That's the way the cookie crumbles."**
That's the way life is.

122. "She **spilled the beans**."
She upset the plans by accidentally letting a secret out.

■ Beans are supposed to stay in the pot until they're ready to be served. A secret is supposed to stay hidden until it's ready to be revealed. If you spill the beans out of the pot, that's like telling a secret.

123. "That's just a **red herring**."
That's meant to mislead us and throw us off the track.

■ Years ago escaped prisoners being chased by the police used an old trick to mislead their pursuers. They dragged a dried red herring behind them to leave a false scent that confused the bloodhounds. The trick often worked!

124. "She's a **big cheese**. He's the **top banana**."
They're both important, influential people.

125. "He's calling it **sour grapes** now."
He wanted something but couldn't get it, so now he says he wouldn't have liked it even if he had gotten it.

■ Aesop told a fable about a fox on a hot day who wanted to munch on a bunch of luscious-looking grapes hanging from a vine. He tried and tried, but he couldn't reach them. Naturally he was extremely annoyed. To make himself feel better he said that the grapes were probably sour anyway.

·6·

Hats

The last thing you put on when you go out and the first thing you take off when you come in is often your hat. Hats have been the sign of importance for centuries. You could tell a lot about a person by the size and style of his crown or cap.

The following play is filled with hat idioms to cap our collection of confusing expressions. Read the play by yourself or aloud with some friends. See if you can figure out what the eleven famous hat idioms mean. The explanations are given at the end of the play.

> **THE BOY WHO HATED HATS**
> **and how he finally bought the perfect one**
> A play in one act using a hatful of hat idioms

Scene: In a hat store.
Characters: Hattie, the hatter   Hal, the hatter
                  Harry, the hatter   Harold Nohat
                  Mrs. Nohat, Harold's mother

Hattie:	Hold on to your hats!
Hal and Harry:	What is it?
Hattie:	Mrs. Nohat is coming toward our store with her son Harold.
Hal and Harry:	So?
Hattie:	Harold hates hats. He won't wear one.
Hal:	He won't take off his big stereo earphones.
Hattie:	The antennas are so high, he can't put a hat on.
Harry:	I'll sell him a hat. I can sell anything to anyone.
Hattie:	You're just talking through your hat.
Harry:	I'm the greatest hat salesman in the world.
Hal:	Oh, don't act so high hat.
Harry:	Just watch me. I'll do it.
Hal:	If you do, I'll eat my hat.
Hattie:	You're as mad as a hatter, Harry.
Harry:	I am a hatter!
Hal and Hattie:	That's why! *(Harold and his mother enter.)*

Harold:	Why are you dragging me into this store, Mother?
Mrs. Nohat:	To get you a hat, Harold.
Harry:	Yes, madam. What can I do for you?
Harold:	Can't you guess? Put on your thinking cap.
Harry:	Would you like to see something in a hat, madam?
Mrs. Nohat:	Yes. My son's head. And no old-fashioned styles.

Hal:	Oh, no, madam. We have nothing old hat in this store.
Harry:	I have the perfect hat for you, young man.
Harold:	No hat's perfect for me. I'm the boy who hates hats.
Harry:	*(Takes a hat out of a box.)* Oh, but I'm sure you'll like this one, young man. *(Whispers in Harold's ear.)*

Harold:	That's perfect for me! I'll wear it now. *(He leaves.)*
Mrs. Nohat:	I don't believe it! How much is the hat?
Harry:	Fifty dollars.
Mrs. Nohat:	*(Paying)* I have no money left. How will I buy lunch?
Hattie:	You'll have to pass the hat.
Hal:	There are plenty of them around here! *(Mrs. Nohat leaves.)*
Hal & Hattie:	You did it! You sold him a hat!
Hal:	That's really a feather in your cap, Harry.
Hattie:	How did you do it?
Harry:	I showed him a hat with built-in stereo earphones, so he can have his hat and wear it, too!
Hal and Hattie:	Great idea! Our hats are off to you!
Harry:	Now that you know the secret, keep it under your hat.

The End

Explanations

126. **"Hold on to your hat!"**
Prepare yourself for some astounding news that will amaze you.

127. "You're **talking through your hat**."
You don't know what you're talking about. You're saying foolish things.

128. "Don't act so **high hat**."
Don't act so snooty and superior.

■ Long ago, people in high society wore high hats. They were like the judges who wore big wigs or the aristocrats who rode high horses. Today a person acting "high hat" must think he's somebody really important. But he's not such a bigwig and should get down off his high horse.

129. "If you do that, I'll **eat my hat**."
     That'll really be amazing! I'll admit I was wrong.

130. "You're **as mad as a hatter**."
     You're crazy.

     ■ At the tea party in *Alice in Wonderland*, there was a "mad hatter" who acted crazy.

131. "Put on your **thinking cap**."
     Think about this problem carefully and try to figure it out.

     ■ There was an old legend about King Eric XIV of Sweden. He was supposed to have owned a magic cap. Every time he put it on, it gave him special powers. Your brainpower is your "thinking cap." Just put it on when you have some serious thinking to do. No magic, but it often works!

132. "I'd like nothing **old hat**."
Nothing old-fashioned or out of style, please.

133. "You'll have to **pass the hat**."
You'll have to go around asking people for money.

134. "That's **a feather in your cap**."
That's an accomplishment to be proud of.

    ■ In the old days, warriors often put a feather in their helmets for every enemy soldier they defeated on the battlefield. American Indians added feathers to their headdresses as tokens of their conquests. Today you can put a "feather in your cap" for any outstanding achievement.

135. "**Hats off** to you!"
Congratulations!

136. "Keep this **under your hat**."
Don't tell this secret. Keep it hidden.

Here is an alphabetical list of the idioms featured in this book.

Other Books About Idioms

American English Idioms by Harry Collis, Passport Books, Lincolnwood, Illinois, 1986.

Colloquial English by Harry Collis, Regents Publishing Company, Inc., New York, 1981.

Concise Dictionary of English Idioms by William Freeman, third edition, revised and edited by Brian Phythian, The Writer, Inc., Boston, Massachusetts, 1978.

Dictionary of American Idioms by Maxine Tull Boatner and John Edward Gates, Barron's Educational Series, Inc., Woodbury, New York, 1975.

Handbook of American Idioms and Idiomatic Usage by Harold C. Whitford and Robert J. Dixson, Regents Publishing Company, Inc., New York, 1973.

Handy Book of Commonly Used American Idioms by Solomon Wiener, Regents Publishing Company, Inc., New York, 1981.

Heavens to Betsy and Other Curious Sayings by Charles Earle Funk, Harper & Row, New York, 1955.

A Hog on Ice and Other Curious Expressions by Charles Earle Funk, Harper & Row, New York, 1948.

In a Pickle and Other Funny Idioms by Marvin Terban, Clarion Books, New York, 1983.

The Pocket Dictionary of American Slang compiled by Harold Wentworth and Stuart Berg Flexner, Pocket Books, New York, 1968.